WOMEN IN THE WORLD OF AFRICA

WOMEN'S ISSUES:
GLOBAL TRENDS

WOMEN'S ISSUES: GLOBAL TRENDS

WOMEN IN THE WORLD OF AFRICA

BY
JOAN ESHERICK

Mason Crest Publishers
Philadelphia

Mason Crest Publishers Inc.
370 Reed Road
Broomall, Pennsylvania 19008
(866) MCP-BOOK (toll free)

First printing
1 2 3 4 5 6 7 8 9 10

Library of Congress Cataloging-in-Publication Data

Esherick, Joan.
  Women in the world of Africa / by Joan Esherick.
    p. cm. — (Women's issues)
  Includes index.
  ISBN 1-59084-857-8   ISBN 1-59084-856-X (series)
  1. Women—Africa—Juvenile literature. I. Title. II. Series.
  HQ1787.E84 2005
  305.4'096—dc22
                    2004011823

Interior design by Michelle Bouch and MK Bassett-Harvey.
Illustrations by Michelle Bouch.
Produced by Harding House Publishing Service, Inc.
Cover design by Benjamin Stewart.
Printed in India.

CONTENTS

INTRODUCTION

by Mary Jo Dudley

The last thirty years have been a time of great progress for women around the world. In some countries, especially where women have more access to education and work opportunities, the relationships between women and men have changed radically. The boundaries between men's roles and women's roles have been crossed, and women are enjoying many experiences that were denied them in past centuries.

But there is still much to be done. On the global stage, women are increasingly the ones who suffer most from poverty. At the same time that they produce 75 to 90 percent of the world's food crops, they are also responsible for taking care of their households. According to the United Nations, in no country in the world do men come anywhere near to spending as much time on housework as women do. This means that women's job opportunities are often extremely limited, contributing to the "feminization of poverty."

In fact, two out of every three poor adults are women. According to the Decade of Women, "Women do two-thirds of the world's work, receive 10 percent of the world's income, and own one percent of the means of production." Women often have no choice but to take jobs that lack long-term security or

adequate pay; many women work in dangerous working conditions or in unprotected home-based industries. This series clearly illustrates how historic events and contemporary trends (such as war, conflicts, and migration) have also contributed to women's loss of property and diminished access to resources.

A recent report from Human Rights Watch indicates that many countries continue to deny women basic legal protections. Amnesty International points out, "Governments are not living up to their promises under the Women's Convention to protect women from discrimination and violence such as rape and female genital mutilation." Many nations—including the United States—have not ratified the United Nations' Women's Treaty.

During times of armed conflict, especially under policies of ethnic cleansing, women are particularly at risk. Murder, torture, systematic rape, forced pregnancy and forced abortions are all too common human rights violations endured by women around the world. This series presents the experience of women in Vietnam, Cambodia, the Middle East, and other war torn regions.

In the political arena, equality between men and women has still not been achieved. Around the world, women are underrepresented in their local and national governments; on average, women represent only 10 percent of all legislators worldwide. This series provides excellent examples of key female leaders who have promoted women's rights and occupied unique leadership positions, despite historical contexts that would normally have shut them out from political and social prominence.

The Fourth World Conference on Women called upon the international community to take action in the following areas of concern:

- the persistent and increasing burden of poverty on women
- inequalities and inadequacies in access to education and training
- inequalities and inadequacies in access to health care and related services
- violence against women

- the effects of armed or other kinds of conflict on women
- inequality in economic structures and policies, in all forms of productive processes, and in access to resources
- insufficient mechanisms at all levels to promote the advancement of women
- lack of protection of women's human rights
- stereotyping of women and inequality in women's participation in all community systems, especially the media
- gender inequalities in the management of natural resources and the safeguarding of the environment
- persistent discrimination against and violation of the rights of female children

The Conference's mission statement includes these sentences: "Equality between women and men is a matter of human rights and a condition for social justice and is also a necessary and fundamental prerequisite for equality, development and peace. . . equality between women and men is a condition . . . for society to meet the challenges of the twenty-first century." This series provides examples of how women have risen above adversity, despite their disadvantaged social, economic, and political positions.

Each book in WOMEN'S ISSUES: GLOBAL TRENDS takes a look at women's lives in a different key region or culture, revealing the history, contributions, triumphs, and challenges of women around the world. Women play key roles in shaping families, spirituality, and societies. By interweaving historic backdrops with the modern-day evolving role of women in the home and in society at large, this series presents the important part women play as cultural communicators. Protection of women's rights is an integral part of universal human rights, peace, and economic security. As a result, readers who gain understanding of women's lives around the world will have deeper insight into the current condition of global interactions.

"WHAT HAS BEEN BLOWN AWAY CANNOT BE FOUND AGAIN." —AFRICAN PROVERB (KENYA)

WOMEN IN AFRICAN HISTORY

At the tender age of seventeen, she lost her father to an early death. According to custom, she coinherited her father's throne with her brother, and she expected they would rule together. Her power-hungry sibling, however, didn't want to share his reign, so he betrayed her and sent her out of the country. She gathered an army and tried to retake the place that was rightfully hers, but failed. At twenty-one years of age, still desperate to retake her throne, she rolled herself in a carpet and presented herself disguised as a gift to a mighty warrior and ruler of a distant land. The great leader, intrigued by the exiled queen's creativity, fell in love with her, and the two joined forces to overthrow her brother and reclaim her throne. They succeeded.

Who were these two conniving souls? Cleopatra and Julius Caesar.

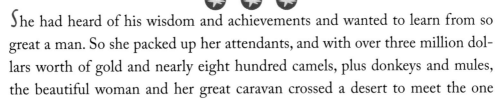

She had heard of his wisdom and achievements and wanted to learn from so great a man. So she packed up her attendants, and with over three million dollars worth of gold and nearly eight hundred camels, plus donkeys and mules, the beautiful woman and her great caravan crossed a desert to meet the one

A woman in Nigeria pounds grain for her family's food.

WOMEN IN THE WORLD OF AFRICA

about whom she'd heard so much. Overwhelmed by her gifts and impressed by her intellect and beauty, the man of wisdom made the young woman feel at home when she arrived. He welcomed her graciously and received her offerings. He built a special apartment where she could live while she remained in his land. He held banquets in her honor and showered her with gifts. He invited her to discuss her questions with him and allowed her to accompany him throughout his kingdom while he held court, ruled his subjects, and settled their disputes. The two valued each other's knowledge and hunger for learning, and both developed reputations for being very wise.

Who were these two people of wisdom beyond their years? Israel's King Solomon and Makeda, Queen of Sheba.

The partnerships we see in these two entries from Africa's ancient history— Cleopatra and Julius Caesar, and the Queen of Sheba and King Solomon— sound remarkably modern: men and women corulers; men and women students of wisdom; men and women heads of state; men and women leaders of war. Does that surprise you? It might, if you envision Africa as a place where women are routinely oppressed and have been for generations. But history paints a different picture. Africa hasn't always been the place of oppression we hear about today.

Anthropologists suggest that early African women worked side-by-side with men to ensure their families' survival. Each person in the family had a necessary role to play. As Simiyu Wandibba, professor of anthropology at the University of Nairobi, notes in a BBC commentary on ancient civilizations in Africa:

> they lived in small family groups, and . . . each family would have its own residential unit. The men would go out to hunt, and the women would have gone out to collect vegetable foods—roots, fruits, nuts and insects—

that formed an important component of the diet. We know that boys were taught to become hunters and the girls gatherers.

In ancient Africa, women seem to have been less *subservient* to men than in later civilizations. They appear to have been coworkers in providing daily necessities. The daily need to find food, water, and shelter meant that each gender simply had a different role to fill. And as their families' needs changed, so did their roles.

Archaeologists tell us that the earliest Africans were *nomadic* hunters and gatherers; they traveled from place to place in search of game, water, and wild plants to eat. But as their populations increased, and as game numbers dwindled, the African people adapted and became more agriculturally based. They learned to farm and grow crops to supplement their hunting expeditions. They built small villages and moved less often. They began raising livestock including cattle, sheep, and goats. These changes impacted the roles of women as much as they did the roles of men.

Instead of gathering, women began to plant, tend, and harvest crops. They learned to grow grain and make breads from certain grains. They still gathered roots and berries growing near their villages, but traveled less. The women took care of the children, did the cooking, gathered wood, fetched water, tended the fires, and kept their dwellings clean. The men still hunted, trained the boys, and made up warring parties, but they too traveled less. Depending on culture, sometimes the men watched over and cared for any livestock the tribe or family owned. In others, women cared for the goats, sheep, and cattle.

This Africa—the Africa of ages past—is the Africa we readily envision: primitive, agricultural, and nomadic. Open fires, game hunts, tribal warriors, ritual dances, nakedness—these are the things many people think of when they think of Africa, even today. But thinking of African people as backward or primitive denies the rich, civilized history of Africa's more recent past.

A modern African woman.

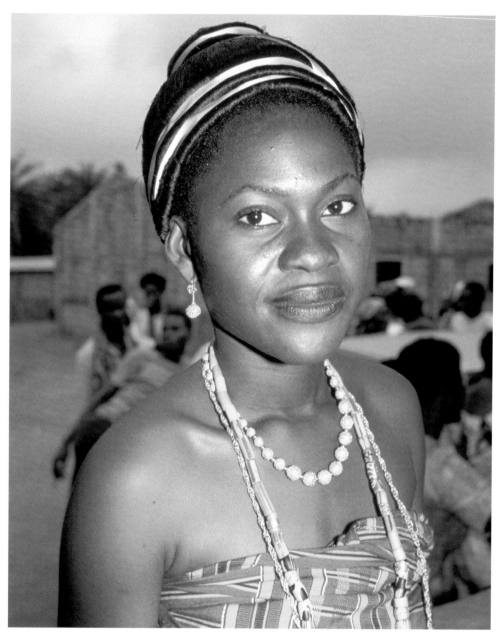

Africans have a rich and sophisticated cultural heritage. This Ashanti woman wears the traditional attire of her people.

Despite the widespread misconceptions we hold of her today, the African continent is the birthplace of civilized society. George Abungu, Director-General of the National Museums of Kenya, explains: "So far the evidence that we have in the world points to Africa as the Cradle of Humankind." The world's first peoples lived there. The world's first civilizations developed there. Some of the world's earliest and greatest advances occurred there. Think of the architecture used to build the marvel we know as the Great Pyramids of Egypt or the engineering skill behind the dams, canals, and dikes developed to keep the great Nile River from flooding cities each year.

Engineering and architectural feats weren't the only advancements of early Africa. Many early African nations used complicated systems of law that protected and ruled their citizens, including women. Laws of ancient Egypt allowed women to own land, bequeath land to heirs, inherit land, own and operate businesses, testify in court, and own other property, including slaves. Egypt's legal system protected free Egyptian women (not slaves) almost as equally as men.

Other cultures in Africa developed advanced, stable governments like those used in Egypt, including her southern neighbor, Kush (today's southern Egypt and northern Sudan). The people of Kush, called Nubians, elected their kings and revered their queens. In ancient civilizations, as we saw in this chapter's opening accounts of Cleopatra and the Queen of Sheba, women sometimes held positions of great power and influence.

So what happened? Why did women's influence and power decline over the centuries? Some historians suggest rural tribal customs, which viewed women as property and of less value than men, gained more influence as the great urban civilizations declined. Others say that women, in general, never really had power on the African continent; only a privileged few held positions of influence, like those women born to royal families. Still others would say that inva-

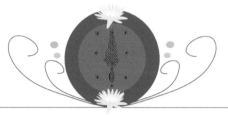

A FEW GREAT WOMEN FROM AFRICA'S PAST

Hatshepsut (1503–1482 B.C.): female warrior and Pharaoh of Kemet (ancient Egypt)

Tiye (1415–1340 B.C.): Nubian-born Queen of Kemet (ancient Egypt)

Nefertari (1292–1225 B.C.): Queen of Kemet (ancient Egypt), wife and great love of Ramses II, Pharaoh

Candace (332 B.C.): Empress of Ethiopia known for military expertise

Cleopatra VII (69–30 B.C.): Queen of Kemet (ancient Egypt) who overthrew her treacherous brother's reign and aided Julius Caesar

Amina (A.D. 1533–1589): Nigerian queen known for military achievements

Nzingha (A.D. 1582–1663): also known as Jinga and Ginga, Queen of Matamba West Africa who resisted European slave traders

Nehanda (nineteenth century): grandmother of Zimbabwe who resisted English colonization

sion by foreign countries and subsequent colonization (becoming an official colony of the foreign invaders) brought new practices of inequality between men and women to African lands. Some even suggest that the spread of a religion that viewed God as male, or used male terminology for God and viewed

men as having higher authority than women (Judaism, Christianity, and Islam), accounted for the decline of women in many African societies.

No matter how you look at the roles of women in Africa's past or present, no single image or answer will adequately explain the changes women experienced throughout the centuries. Africa is too big a continent, with too many countries and too many types of people and cultures, for one explanation to do. Just as the roles and history of American women differ depending on culture, heritage, era, social status, educational opportunities, family values, religion, and other factors, so the history and roles of African women vary from woman to woman, depending on myriad influences. There is no such thing as a "typical American"—and there is no such thing as a "typical African" either.

Africa is truly a melting pot of languages, customs, skin colors, traditions, beliefs, nations, and governments. To understand the women of Africa then, we have to understand their basic differences.

AFRICA: BASIC INFORMATION

Today, many agencies list fifty-four nations in Africa, though not everyone agrees on that number. The United Nations lists only fifty-three African member states, but not all countries seek membership in the United Nations. Additional reasons for the disagreement are that some countries are waging war, others contest their boundaries (and names), and still others are further defining their independence. To make things even more complicated, while nations are important, African people as a whole tend to identify most with their cultures, tribes, or heritages, rather than their nations. It would be like someone in the United States introducing himself to a foreigner by saying, "I'm an East Coast Protestant," or "I'm a Southerner," or "I'm a Californian," rather than saying, "I'm an American."

To make it easier to discuss various women in this book, we'll look at women from certain nations, but we'll also discuss Africa by regions rather

SOME AFRICAN TRIBES AND PEOPLE GROUPS

Berber: African people (dating back several centuries) who live in several northern countries including Morocco, Algeria, Tunisia, Libya, and Egypt

Bobo: an agricultural people known for intricate masks and elaborate ceremonial clothes

Bushmen: the oldest inhabitants of southern Africa (dating back 20,000 years) who live in the Kalahari Desert.

Dogon: cliff-dwellers of southeastern Mali and Burkina Faso

Fulani: largest nomadic group in the world, primarily herders and traders

Kikuyu (Gikuyu): Kenya's largest ethnic group

Maasai: famous herders and warriors who once dominated East African plains and can be identified by their bright red draped clothing

Pygmies: a "catch-all" term for various pygmy types, including the Bambuti, the Batwa, and the Bayaka, who live in central and western Africa

Taureg: nomadic people of the Sahara desert

Wolof: one of the largest people groups to inhabit modern-day Senegal

Yoruba: an artistic people of southwest Nigeria and Benin known for their pottery, weaving, beadwork, metalwork, and mask making

Zulu: South Africa's largest ethnic group, well known for small carvings and brightly colored beads and baskets

than national boundaries. The continent is usually divided into these basic regions:

1. North Africa (includes six countries): Algeria, Egypt, Libya, Morocco, Tunisia, Western Sahara (Morocco claims this country).
2. East Africa (includes ten countries): Comoros, Djibouti, Eritrea, Ethiopia, Kenya, Madagascar, Seychelles, Somalia, Sudan, Uganda (this region can also include Mauritius, Tanzania, Burundi, and Rwanda).
3. Southern Africa (includes twelve countries): Angola, Botswana, Lesotho, Malawi, Mauritius, Mozambique, Namibia, South Africa, Swaziland, Tanzania, Zambia, Zimbabwe.
4. Central Africa (includes ten countries): Burundi, Cameroon, Central African Republic, Chad, Congo (Brazzaville), Congo (Kinshasa), Equatorial Guinea, Gabon, Rwanda, São Tomé and Príncipe.
5. West Africa (includes sixteen countries): Benin, Burkina Faso, Cape Verde, Côte d'Ivoire (Ivory Coast), Gambia, Ghana, Guinea (Conakry), Guinea (Bissau), Liberia, Mali, Mauritania, Niger, Nigeria, Senegal, Sierra Leone, Togo.

AFRICA'S REGIONS

The region in which a woman lives can determine much about her history, health, and overall status. Other factors influence the lives of African women, too.

World atlas statistics (based on the CIA World Factbook) cite over 800 million people living on this continent. (That's nearly three times as many people as are living in the United States.) The continent includes the world's largest desert (the Sahara), the world's longest river (the Nile), and one of the world's highest peaks (Mt. Kilimanjaro). Its environments include tropical rain forests,

North Africa

Morocco
Tunisia
Algeria
Libya
Egypt

Western
Sahara

East Africa

Cape
Verde

Mauritania
Mali
Niger
Chad
Sudan
Eritrea
Djibouti
Ethiopia

Senegal
Gambia
Guinea Bissau
Guinea
Sierra Leone
Ivory
Coast
Ghana
Libera
Togo
Benin
Nigeria

Cameroon
Central
African Republic

Equatorial Guinea
Sao Tome & Principe
Gabon
R. of Congo
D.R. of Congo
Rwanda
Burundi
Uganda
Kenya
Somalia

West Africa

Seychelles

Central Africa

Comoros

Tanzania

Madagascar

Angola
Zambia
Malawi

Namibia
Zimbabwe
Mauritius

Botswana
Mozambique

Southern Africa
Swaziland
Lesotho
South Africa

lush green highlands, desert regions, above-the-tree-line snow regions, swamps, plains, coastal wetlands, and *savannahs*. Its climate can be arid, hot, drought-ridden, or inundated with flooding downpours during rainy seasons. Its landscapes include vast stretches of untamed wilderness, national parks, remote villages, rural farmlands, urban centers, active shipping ports, and bustling cities. Its roadways can be paved or dirt, easily passed or nearly impassable.

Africa's people, like her terrain, are diverse. Her women come with many faces, experiences, heartaches, and joys. They come from many places, tongues, skin colors, tribes, and cultures. According to TeacherLink USA (an online educational resource for teachers), over a thousand languages are used in Africa today. The continent boasts nearly as many tribes (the nation of Zambia has over seventy tribes all by itself). And every tribe has its own set of customs and laws regarding women. These differ even from their national laws. You can see how any discussion of African women becomes complicated with so many influences involved!

Obviously, no two African women are alike. Each has her own dreams and limitations. Each has rules by which she must live. But each is an individual with a value, worth, and dignity all her own.

"TWO SMALL ANTELOPES CAN BEAT A BIG ONE."—AFRICAN PROVERB (IVORY COAST)

2

AFRICAN WOMEN TODAY

Half the buttons on Nophiwa Sinquina's skirt have fallen off, and despite the long distances she walks, her shoes are only floppy sneakers. But Sinquina . . . has something many young people here, especially young women, envy: a job.

A few times a month, the quiet, young woman leads visitors along South Africa's eastern shore as part of a community-run tourism project. Visitors around the world come to see the area's rugged beauty, but for the people of Pondoland—named for the rural Xhosa-speaking Pondo people who live here—life here is hard. (From WeNews correspondent Nicole Itano's article "Africa's Future May Depend on Women's Employment," 02/08/04.)

My name is Salma. I was born a slave in Mauritania in 1956. My parents were slaves, and their parents were slaves of the same family. As soon as I was old enough to walk, I was forced to work all day, every day. Even if we were sick, we had to work.

When I was still a child, I started taking care of the first wife of the head of the family and her fifteen children. . . . I was beaten very often with a wooden stick or leather belt. One day they were beating my mother, and I couldn't stand it. I tried to stop them. The head of the family got very angry with me.

A trader in the Nigerian swamplands.

He tied my hands, and branded me with a burning iron, and hit me across the face. His ring cut my face and left a scar. (From a first-person account in "21st Century Slaves," *National Geographic*, September 2003.)

The nomad's life is a harsh one, but it is also full of beauty. . . . My mother named me after a miracle of nature: Waris means desert flower. The desert flower blooms in a barren environment where few living things can survive. Sometimes it doesn't rain in a country for over a year. But finally the water pours down, cleansing the dusty landscape, and then like a miracle the blooms appear. . . .

When a girl marries, the women from her tribe go out into the desert and collect these flowers. They dry them, then add water to them and make a paste to spread on the bride's face that gives her a golden glow. . . . Maybe they don't own much; many families are incredibly poor, but there is no shame over this fact. She'll simply wear the best she or her mother or sisters or friends can find, and carry herself with fierce pride—a trait all Somalis bear. By the time her wedding day comes, she walks out to greet her groom as a stunning beauty. (From *Desert Flower* by Waris Dirie and Cathleen Miller.)

"Nobody cares if we live or die," said forty-five-year old Samira Hassan. *"We have lived here [in Cairo, Egypt] for thirty-five years. The city promised us electricity and water. We paid for electricity to be installed five years ago. They took our money—we still have the receipt—but they never came back."* Samira has never left the community, never visited a park or seen the countryside. *"We can't have time, we don't have money. I tried to grow a flower once, but nothing green grows here.*

Samira is a mother of nine. "I had six more children but they died when they were very young. It is common here. We have many problems—scorpions, mosquitoes, rats, and [weasels]. . . . They bite our babies, feed off them, in the night. Children get sick, fevers, and then they die. In the winter, the roofs leak, it is very cold at night, more children die. (From *Price of Honor* by Jan Goodwin.)

Sierra Leone is a country where women have always been very organized through their professional groups and their secret and ritual societies. Women are used to working in groups that are very influential. . . . In 1995 we women embarked on a new campaign for the return of an elected, civilian government, which we believed would move [the country] forward. . . . But just two weeks before the elections, the military government announced that it intended to postpone [the elections]. And for the first time we women entered into direct confrontation with the military government. We organized another march . . . we went to the National Consultative Assembly to lobby the delegates. We went there clad in black to show our . . . mourning for our hoped-for democracy. Women went in huge numbers and fought with the soldiers who tried to stop them from attending. After a very heated debate, the decision was made to go ahead with the elections. Women [acted] as presiding officers and election observers, and [mobilized] people to vote. After the vote, women stayed in the polling stations to protect the ballot boxes and materials against intruders who, we feared, would come overnight and take them away. (From Yasmin Fofanah's testimony to the United Nations Development Fund for Women [UNIFEM] in their publication *The Impact of War and Reconstruction on Women's Access to Land and Property.*)

Each of the women in these paragraphs is African. One is a tour guide, a single woman earning her way. One endured modern-day slavery until she escaped her native land. The third, who grew up as a nomad in the African desert, works as a world-famous model whose face appears in national and international women's magazines. And the last two represent extremes for modern women: one dwells in urban slums outside of Cairo and seems resigned to her fate; the other is a political *activist* working toward change. Five different women; five sets of life circumstances; five countries, one continent: Africa.

Who is today's African woman? All of these women represent her. Yet, none provides a complete picture. No typical "African" woman exists. Some African women live in rural settings and some in urban developments. Some pursue

Maasai children.

higher education; others cannot even read. Some work in professions; some stay home. Some marry (or are married off by their families); some fight to remain single. Some bear children; others remain childless. Some live long lives; others die young. As with the rest of the world, some women will represent Africa in the next Olympic Games, while others will die from AIDS (Acquired Immune

An Ashanti woman.

Deficiency Syndrome) even before the next games can begin. A rare few, like the queens who came before them, will become famous, serve in government, or lead their nations. Many more will grow up, marry, raise children, and die without anyone but a few close relatives knowing their names.

No, there is no such thing as a typical African woman, but many African women share similar challenges and privileges today. One necessary trait of contemporary women in Africa is flexibility: the willingness to change. Kenyan writer Rebeka Njau's description of Maasai women in her native land illustrates the need for flexibility in today's Africa. Her account in "Learning to Grow," published by New Internationalist, June 1990, is adapted here:

Kipiku Kuyan and the other Maasai women suffered terribly when drought struck Kenya during the early 1980s. Wells and streams dried up. Cows and goats roamed the plains devouring any leaves available. Soon the hungry animals had eaten everything. One by one they started to die.

Kipiku and her family trekked miles seeking water and green pasture for their few remaining cows and goats. But everywhere it was the same: Intensive grazing had left the land bare and uninhabitable.

Life was grim for the Maasai, who depended on cattle for food. Their children were riddled with skin ailments, sick with diarrhea, and stick-legged from malnutrition. Government and voluntary organizations made frantic efforts to supply them with food.

It was a humiliating experience.

Kipiku had to do something. She recalled a Maasai woman who had started a small homestead along a stream and seemed able to feed her children. The woman, Lois Nkurne, belonged to an organization that promoted development among women in the rural areas; the organization was called the Women's Development Committee.

Kipiku took some friends to pay Lois a visit. She wanted to learn how this woman had improved her family's quality of life.

Lois advised the women to start a self-help group to produce food and generate income. They did so, forming a group of seventy women. They started growing food, working secretly without consulting their men. Cultivation was new to the women, but with Lois's help, the group harvested a reasonable crop of cabbages, onions, tomatoes, and a green vegetable called sukuma wiki.

Next the group learned how to irrigate the land. Then they planted beans, potatoes, and *pawpaws*. When the vegetables had sprouted, the women proudly took them to show the committee what they had achieved. To their surprise the committee gave them more land to cultivate.

One major difficulty had been getting irrigation supplies, but the women started a handicraft *cooperative* to raise money for irrigation pipes. They made beadwork and leather goods to sell at local tourist markets.

Today their men treat them differently. "The men value women now, because of their knowledge, effort and initiative," says Kipiku.

The Maasai in this account had to adapt or die. Their flexibility and willingness to learn new skills allowed them to survive and prosper in their changing land.

African woman throughout the continent face similar changes, great and small. Some, like those in Sudan, live in the midst of extreme drought. Others, like those in Somalia, the Democratic Republic of Congo, and Rwanda, have lived through terrible wars. More seem to be living through incredible transitions from agricultural rural environments to modernization. The United Nations documents the status of these women—their challenges and privileges—in a periodically released publication called *The World's Women: Trends and Statistics.*

When crises hit, women and children often suffer the most.

THE UNITED NATIONS' ASSESSMENT OF WOMEN IN THE WORLD TODAY

The *World's Women 2000* cites some encouraging worldwide trends, which also represent trends in many African nations:

- On average, women are having fewer, but healthier children.
- Women are generally marrying at older ages (twenties instead of teens).
- In most regions, life expectancy has increased for women.
- Girls are catching up to boys in schooling opportunities.
- Women have made significant gains in higher education.
- More women are entering the workforce than ever before.

But the news isn't all good. Several statistics raise alarms about the situation of women in Africa:

- In certain developing countries (many in Africa), more than a quarter of women aged fifteen to nineteen are already married.
- Life expectancy in Southern Africa has decreased dramatically because of AIDS.
- In countries with high rates of HIV/AIDS, women account for more than half of all AIDS cases and are at greater risk for getting the disease than are men.
- In some African countries, women still lag behind men in education.
- Nearly six hundred million women in the world cannot read or write.
- Women experience more unemployment than men for longer periods.

We'll address some of the key issues facing today's African women in the last chapter of this book, but for now these statistics reveal that women in Africa

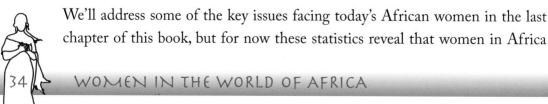

face a mix of positive gains and frustrating challenges. The difference in a woman's life comes with her family's expectations, social customs, and tribal or religious laws. It also comes with her level of isolation.

An African proverb says, "Two small antelopes can beat a big one." As Yasmin Fofanah (whose testimony is recorded earlier in this chapter) discovered, women working together can accomplish much for each other. In her case, two small antelopes (a group of women) did indeed beat a big one (the military government who sought to shut the elections down). The proverb from the Ivory Coast proved true in her situation. Will it for other women in Africa?

"A HOME WITHOUT A WOMAN IS LIKE A BARN WITHOUT CATTLE."—AFRICAN PROVERB (ETHIOPIA)

AFRICAN WOMEN IN THE FAMILY

A coworker at the university where I worked invited me to dinner at his house and told me he would arrive to pick me up at six o'clock. Six o'clock came and went. Then seven, then eight. By eight-thirty, I assumed Philippe, my intended dinner companion, was working late and had simply forgotten about dinner. At nine-thirty I heard his horn outside and pressed the security button to release the driveway gate; the gate opened, and his car pulled in. Philippe jumped out of his small sedan. Grinning from ear to ear, he greeted me with, "I am here to pick you up for dinner."

He didn't explain why he was late. He didn't apologize. He didn't even acknowledge that he'd been inconsiderate in keeping me waiting. I was annoyed, but I managed to greet him with a smile. As an American working in Kenya, I'd learned to set aside my feelings in this sometimes strange land.

Philippe, a refugee from a rural village in Burundi, now lived in Kenya where he'd earned a Ph.D. and several other degrees. Highly educated, he lectured at the local university where I worked and directed a regional ministry office. His

compassion and concern for others immediately attracted me to him, so I'd accepted his invitation to meet his family at dinner without question.

When we reached his home, his entire family came outside to greet us: his wife, sons and daughters, and mother. He lived in a comfortable townhouse in a middle-class Nairobi neighborhood. A spacious living/dining area greeted us as we walked through the door. Savory smells of rice, chicken, fish, stew, and other dishes wafted through the room.

I sat in the living room with Philippe, his friends, and the men of the family. The women remained in the kitchen. We discussed university business, his professional plans, Kenyan politics, and my observations about Africa after having lived in Nairobi for just over a year. I found it odd that I sat as the lone woman among men, but they seemed genuinely interested in and appreciative of my views.

The women finally appeared with the food: serving, waiting on us, delivering seconds and thirds to the men as they wished. None sat with us for conversation.

Because I'd worked with Philippe for several months, and we'd developed a certain friendship, I found the courage to ask about the absent women. "When do your wife and daughters eat?"

He smiled. "When we are done, they will eat what is left."

The women got leftovers! I couldn't believe it. This wasn't some backward African; Philippe spent years pursuing higher education. He'd studied in modern universities in foreign countries overseas. He respected me as a peer, enjoyed our professional discussions, and seemed to respect my credentials.

When I asked about his daughter's schooling, he told me about his sons. When I pressed further, he explained, "In our culture only boys need an education; girls learn women's work. I will arrange my daughter's marriage when she comes of age and then she won't need an education. Her husband will take care of her, just as it's always been."

Some Africans make their living collecting and selling firewood.

Tribal family life in Kenya.

Puzzled, I pressed further. "But where did you meet your wife?"

"Oh, at University, of course. I would never have married an uneducated woman."

This fictionalized account—in part my own experience in Kenya, and in part an experience recounted in *African Insights Ezine Newsletter* (July 2002)—illus-

trates the strange *paradox* of women in Africa. On one hand, women are valued as indispensable family members and worthy of great honor, protection, and care. On the other, women don't receive the same encouragement to pursue education or careers as men. Societal norms expect them to remain in the home.

In most parts of Africa, family is by far the most important institution. To be a wife and mother is the highest status many African women can obtain. Men revere women as the keepers of the family and the means by which their names can be carried to future generations.

Family comes first. Family ties are for the most part permanent, and family loyalty is stronger than national or tribal loyalty. Parents teach children to obey their elders from the time they are old enough to understand what it means to obey. Obedience to family norms and expectations is expected and rarely questioned. In societies where family membership can mean life or death (as in sharing food or water or protection from enemies), the worst punishment can be banishment from the family.

Obedience seems like a harsh expectation, but it provides strong family bonds, is designed to benefit the family, and is intended to build trust. These family ties reveal themselves best in family celebrations. Any significant life event—a birth, the naming of a child, rites of passage into adulthood, graduation from school, marriage, death—brings celebrations of various types depending on culture and tribal identity. Food, festive gatherings, dances, song— you name it, it's probably part of some celebration ritual.

For women in Africa, the celebrations that vary the most—and create the most controversy—are the ones that honor moving from girlhood to womanhood and marriage.

GIRLHOOD

Depending on where a girl grows up in Africa, she has certain domestic chores: helping with cooking, cleaning, caring for children, caring for the sick,

caring for aged parents, gardening (planting, tending, harvesting), animal chores (milking, tending flocks, watering), carrying drinking water, gathering firewood, tending the fire, shopping, or trading. Older women will likely teach her customary trades or crafts (weaving, beadwork, sewing, basketry). Sometimes her elders will send her to sell goods at market or to work as a helper in other families.

Many girls, if their families can afford to send them, will also attend at least some level of primary school, although one study estimates that nearly 60 percent of African women receive no further education. Depending on her family's commitment to learning, she may or may not attend secondary school. Most girls never attend college. As the story at the start of this chapter illustrates, the assumption is that girls will simply marry; they don't need educations.

An African girl's childhood is filled with family, chores, some schooling, and childhood games. But her childhood seems brief. However, most African girls don't jump from childhood to marriage without some rite of passage marking her transition from being a child to becoming a marriageable young woman. For some girls, getting her first menses (period) is enough to mark her as ready to marry. For others, ritual prayers, body painting, and dancing announce her eligibility. For still others, a dangerous, often painful surgical procedure called female genital mutilation (FGM) or female circumcision marks her transition to womanhood. Many African girls undergo FGM between the ages of six and twelve.

FEMALE GENITAL MUTILATION/FEMALE CIRCUMCISION

In some African cultures, no self-respecting man will marry a woman who has not been circumcised. Circumcision is supposed to guard a girl's virginity until her wedding night. Sometimes called a "surgical chastity belt," FGM is designed to keep a girl from engaging in sexual intercourse until she is married.

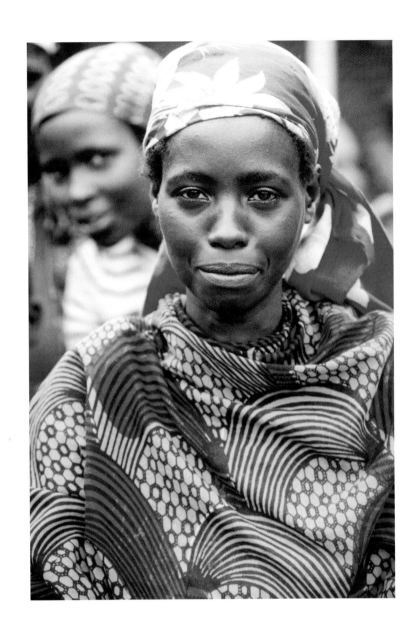

Although outlawed in some countries, FGM remains widespread and acceptable in many cultures, and is practiced in nearly thirty countries in Africa, some with lower rates of practice (for example, only five percent of women in the Democratic Republic of Congo undergo FGM), and some with widespread practice rates (nearly 98 percent of women in Somalia undergo FGM).

FGM procedures vary, but most include removing all or part of the girl's external genitalia (her labia and clitoris) and almost always conclude with the *midwife* sewing the girl's vaginal opening closed, leaving only a tiny opening (about the size of the tip of a matchstick) through which the girl can pass menstrual blood.

Parents feel obligated to arrange circumcisions for their daughters to purify and cleanse them for marriage. According to some mistaken customs, the parts removed during circumcision are "dirty," will cause a girl to act out sexually, and will make the girl smell bad if not removed. According to Hanny Lightfoot-Klein in her work *Prisoners of Ritual*, Kenyan girls from the Kikuyu tribe sing these lyrics after undergoing FGM:

The knife cut down the guardian of the village today.
Now he is dead and gone [referring to the clitoris, clitoral hood, and labia].
Before the village was dirty, but now without the guardian it is clean . . .
Now we can make love, because our sex is clean.

Because they've been circumcised, these girls see themselves as "clean." They see uncircumcised girls as immature or dirty. Like these Kenyan girls, many Africans, especially African men, see FGM surgery as a purifying ritual that guarantees a girl's purity and marriage eligibility.

Sadly, most girls have no say about participating in this brutal, unnecessary procedure, despite its risks (see page 46). Because a visiting midwife performs

the rite in secret, and most circumcised girls won't discuss their experience, young girls know little of what actually happens during the surgery. Many girls even request to be circumcised; they are in a hurry to be accepted by their older friends, sisters, and cousins. Peer pressure plays a large role in this rite. Like dri-

RISKS OF FGM

extreme pain (when done without anesthesia, which is often)

excessive bleeding

shock from pain or blood loss

infection

high fevers from infection

death (from blood loss or infection)

painful urination

inability to urinate (when sewn closed too tightly)

long-term urinary-tract problems

chronic infections

painful menstrual cycles

inability to discharge menstrual blood

painful intercourse

childbirth difficulties

ver's licenses for American youth, circumcision marks adulthood for many African girls. They look forward to the day when they will "become women."

Once the girls heal from their circumcisions, which can take weeks of immobility and pain, they become eligible for marriage proposals. In some countries and cultures, the girls can refuse proposals; in others, they must comply, no matter their age or what they want or feel.

ARRANGED MARRIAGES: OPPORTUNITY OR OPPRESSION?

Marriage in many African nations is not like marriage in America or other Western societies. It isn't marked by romance, dating, or young couples "falling in love." Many African women leave the choice of a lifelong marriage partner to their parents—they really have no other choice. These "arranged" marriages involve negotiations between families of both the bride and groom.

THE LOBOLA

"Lobola" in English means "a set amount paid by a prospective husband to the bride's family among certain peoples in southern Africa." In the Zulu language, it means "bride price."

In Africa, marriage isn't just a contract between one man and one woman; it's an agreement between families (and their clans or tribes). The lobola is the amount senior members of both families agree the groom should pay for the privilege of marrying the bride. Americans think this age-old custom treats the bride as a product to be purchased, while Africans view it (when handled appropriately) as a complicated negotiation marked by growing trust and respect that brings two families together. The more highly the bride is esteemed (considering her age, education, talents, abilities), the higher the lobola. A high bride price brings great honor to the bride and her family.

In rural societies, bride prices include numbers of cattle. Five cows could be considered a high bride price in some cultures, especially where a man's wealth

This woman is the wife of a tribal chief in Kenya.

A SAMPLING OF MINIMUM AGES FOR MARRIAGE

International organizations like UNICEF (the United Nations Children's Fund) and the United Nations Population Fund recommend that eighteen be the minimum age for marriage for boys and girls. Here are some current practices in African nations:

Cameroon: a girl must be fifteen, a boy eighteen.

Ivory Coast: A girl must be fourteen.

Kenya: A girl must be sixteen.

Tanzania: A girl must be fifteen, but may be as young as twelve in special circumstances.

Morocco: The law recently raised a girl's minimum age from fifteen to eighteen.

Ethiopia: Marriages to girls as young as seven or eight are common.

Nigeria (northern states): The average age of marriage for girls is eleven.

is not measured in money but in the amount of livestock or land he owns. In urban societies, the groom more often pays his lobola in cash.

Once the families decide on the lobola, custom dictates that the bride and groom cannot see each other until the wedding day. The bride is allowed to know who her betrothed will be, but she cannot see him or talk with him.

As with any custom or tradition, lobola can be abused. Today, it is hotly debated in various African cultures. Some people want to do away with the practice to avoid potential abuses. Some greedy families have "sold" their daughters to less-than-honorable grooms to pay off family debts or bad business deals. In the worst cases, abusive grooms purchase brides to treat as property. These unfortunate situations are not, according to most Africans, the norm. When handled with appropriate dignity and ceremony, the lobola can create lifelong bonds of trust and respect between the two joining families. And in many cases, the couples grow to love each other deeply after the wedding vows have been said.

Not every couple is so fortunate.

PROBLEMS IN MARRIAGE

In several African cultures (and nations), customs and laws allow men to beat their wives for such offenses as leaving the home without permission, refusing to have sex when the husband asks, neglecting the children, forgetting a task, or burning a meal. A recent World Health Organization study of Zimbabwe women found that more than half of the women surveyed felt women deserved to be beaten in certain circumstances. They see these beatings as corrective discipline.

Uganda's vice president, Specioza Kazibwe, brought attention to the practice of men "disciplining" their wives when she spoke out against the beatings she endured from her husband. Breaking cultural silence, she asked in a public interview, "Why should I continue staying with a man who beats me?"

Older children in Kenya often help care for their younger siblings.

Maasai women in Kenya.

Enduring physical punishment isn't the only marriage problem African women face. Competition from other wives may be even more difficult to bear. Laws in several countries allow men to marry more than one wife. This practice, called polygamy, occurs with or without the first wife's consent, depending on custom. Though the same laws that allow men multiple wives require them to provide equally for the wives and their children, unequal treatment occurs more often than not. Depending on the country in which she resides, a woman in this situation can have no recourse at all, can sue her husband for neglect, or can obtain a quick divorce without shame. It all depends on where and with whom she lives.

African cultures view women in families as everything from *matriarchs* deserving the highest honor and praise to little more than slaves existing for the benefit of men and the birthing of their children. Customs and laws in various African nations allow women different rights, depending on the region in which they live. Some conditions, however, are intolerable by any standard. Some African women, rather than remaining silent, are moving from the family sector into public life to address the worst of these situations.

"SEEING IS DIFFERENT FROM BEING TOLD."—AFRICAN PROVERB (NIGERIA)

4

BEYOND THE FAMILY: BLAZING NEW TRAILS

They are doctors.

They are military officers.

They are government officials.

They are journalists.

They are computer specialists and Internet gurus.

They are television news anchors.

They are authors, poets, engineers, and musicians.

They are teachers, bankers, university professors, and CEOs.

They are athletes and activists, cooks and conquerors, patriots and political prisoners.

Who are they? Women. *African* women.

Though the bleak picture painted in the previous chapters of women confined to lives at home or rural lands is true for many women in African countries, it isn't true for all. Many African women pursue higher education, influential careers, government positions, and advocacy roles. Still others seek to

Many women in Africa still work on their family farms. This woman is cleaning the husks from grain.

better their situations through training and skill development classes taught in their regions. The United Nations Department of Public Education reports phenomenal growth in African women's education:

- In Botswana, literacy classes, functional literacy projects, and distance education programs enroll more women than men.
- In Burkina Faso, *satellite schools*, nonformal education centers, and literacy-training agencies introduced quotas to ensure that 50 percent of students are girls.
- In Senegal, school enrollment rates for girls went up from 35 percent (one out of three) to nearly 53 percent (more than half).
- In Bhutan, 70 percent of nonformal education students are women.
- In Libya more women go abroad for higher education than men.
- In Namibia, 50 percent more women are enrolled in higher education than men.
- In Zambia, local schools introduced *affirmative action* programs in science and technology to encourage female students to participate in these programs.

Education isn't the only gauge of women entering public life. African women are beginning to infiltrate many previously "men-only" arenas. The United Nations reports that more than 25 percent of parliamentary and ministry positions in South Africa belong to women (compared to only 15 percent of the United States' governmental positions).

In 2000, thirty-nine Zambian women staged a peaceful demonstration to protest the rapes and strangling deaths of four young girls. Zambian police promptly arrested the women, but when women's rights organizations protested their arrest, the resulting public international outcry led to their release.

In Uganda, women farmers regularly access information on fair market prices via the Internet at Nabweru Telecenter, where they can link to the Uganda National Council of Science and Technology. This site offers support and advice for small farmers.

In Ethiopia, the United Nations Economic Commission for Africa (ECA), in partnership with the World Bank and Cisco Systems Inc., launched a technology training course for African women. The training course, which trains twenty-five African women per year, covers six months and 280 instructional hours, and it leads to independent certification as a networking associate. The women who finish this program can then lead other young women to pursue higher technology training and businesses.

From politics to governance to social demonstration to small business ventures, women are gaining ground in modern Africa. Even African women in rural areas seem to be improving their lot.

Thirteen-year-old Esiankiki thought she'd never do anything other than what her mother, grandmothers, sisters, and aunts had always done: build and tend the circular dung huts of her people, cook for the men, weave beaded necklaces for ceremonial wear, watch the younger children, and marry a Maasai warrior someday. But an international development agency helped create a market near her village where Maasai women could sell their handcrafts to tourists—and because of her aptitude for math and beadwork, her father allowed her to attend the agency's young *entrepreneur* training program. The bright, quick-learning student caught the attention of agency trainers, and soon, the teenager found herself training other women to manage their handcraft sales.

"I never thought I could have so much responsibility," Esiankiki said. "I thought I would marry and have babies. Now I can have a business and survive on my own."

These young Malinke women have more opportunities than their mothers did.

DIFFERENT COUNTRIES; DIFFERENT OPPORTUNITIES

As we've said throughout this book, not all African women are the same, nor are their opportunities the same. Yes, women in South Africa can own land, but women in Kenya can't inherit land from their husbands or fathers. The rights and privileges of people in each country vary with that country's *constitution* and legal system.

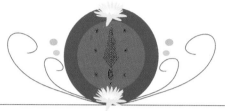

THE MANY SHADES OF AFRICAN WOMEN

African women can live in deserts, green highlands, or cities.

African women can dress in traditional garb or Western-style clothes.

African women can earn Ph.D.s or never even learn to read.

African women can possess strong tribal identities or none at all.

African women can travel worldwide or stay on their tribal lands.

African women can watch television or have no electricity in their homes.

African women can get water from a faucet or from mountain springs.

African women can speak several languages or only their mother tongues.

African women can be dark-skinned, olive-skinned, and many other shades in between.

African women can be shy, outgoing, compliant, or determined.

There is no such thing as a typical African woman.

Apart from these legal inconsistencies, women in many African nations do what women all over the world do. In urban areas they may take public transportation (which may be nothing more than an overloaded pick-up truck), attend religious services, go to restaurants, get active in women's groups, shop at local markets, or enjoy evenings with friends. They may have jobs outside the home, take classes at local schools, or spend time with their spouses and children. In rural settings, when the day's work is done, women might sing, dance, or tell stories of ages past. How a woman behaves in public, and what she can become involved in, depends on the woman's culture, family, and environment.

Tribal customs play significant roles in the expectations and assigned roles of women. Age, marital status, and abilities count, too. Religion can influence a woman's family and public life as well.

"THERE IS NO MEDICINE TO CURE HATRED."—AFRICAN PROVERB (NIGER)

RELIGION AND WOMEN IN AFRICA

An African woman rests by the fireside while her baby cries for nourishment. The young mother, sick with an unknown fever, is too weak to eat anything or to nurse her hungry child. She seems listless and grows weaker with each passing hour. The woman's family calls for the village medicine woman, who arrives, examines the sick woman, and immediately sets off to the fields to look for plants and herbs to use in her medicines. After an hour or so, the old woman returns, mixes her leaves and petals with various liquids from roots she found, and gives her potion to the woman to drink. Several hours pass while the medicine woman waits and watches with concerned relatives. She checks on the young woman, who by then is beginning to respond to her treatment. With a sigh of relief, the healer knows her work is done, yet she returns to check on her patient over the next several days to ensure the recovery in complete. The young mother makes a full recovery, begins nursing her baby again, and both do just fine.

In a different village in another region of Africa, another young woman rests in her family tent, too weak to nurse her newborn child. Instead of calling for a medicine woman, this family calls for the elders of their church to come, anoint the sick woman with oil, and pray for her healing. She too recovers.

In an urban apartment outside of a major city, still another young woman is bed-ridden, too drained from her illness to tend to her nursing infant. Here, her family says ritual prayers to their ancestors, then takes the woman to the local hospital where female doctors treat her illness with modern drugs. Like her rural sisters, she, too, recovers.

WHAT IS AN ANCESTOR?

An ancestor in African religion isn't just someone from which you descended. An ancestor also must meet these criteria:

died a good death

lived faithfully by his laws

transmitted these laws to his children

left many descendents

fostered communication with the dead through sacrifices and prayer

Each of the above scenarios tells the same tale of a young woman too sick to care for her nursing child. In each case, family members seek help and treatment for the sick loved one, and each circumstance yields the same outcome: the young woman recovers. The means of her recovery, however, differ from family to family and from faith to faith.

Religious life in Africa, like every other aspect of African life, is far from *homogenous*. No one religion captures all African hearts; no single faith represents the African religious picture as a whole. Again, women in Africa experience vastly different levels of responsibility, freedom, and respect with regard to their religious roles, depending on the faith of their families and cultures.

In this chapter we'll look at a few key religions in African cultures.

VOODOO

Voodoo isn't as widespread in Africa as many non-Africans think. In some countries, hostile governments banished the religion from public practice. An Associated Press (AP) report headlined the return of Voodoo (also known as Voodoun or Vodun) as a nationally recognized religion in Benin only in 1996, after it was all but abolished by Marxist rulers in the 1970s.

Originating in West Africa four hundred years ago (and in other parts of Africa up to six thousand years ago), Voodoo celebrates spirits called "fetishes," which are said to guide Voodoo worshippers. The AP article describes the celebration of Voodoo's spread through this country, where 60 percent of the people practice this faith:

> Dancers and drummers kept up a spirited pace as alcohol was poured onto the ground as an offering to the gods to ensure peace and prosperity. A similar celebration took place on the beach at Ouidah, twenty-five miles to the west, which is considered the center of Benin's voodoo culture.

The celebration described in the article above illustrates one kind of Voodoo ritual, but Voodoo rituals come in many varieties. Voodoo followers use rituals to make contact with spirits, to gain their favor by offering them animal sacrifices and gifts, or to obtain their help to treat sickness, improve weather situations, or increase family income. Voodoo practitioners will perform rituals after positive events (like marriage, birth, or good fortune), to escape ongoing hardship, to change their "luck," to celebrate Voodoo holidays, or to ask for healing. Though Voodoo followers claim their priests practice only "white magic," some Voodoo priests claim to practice black magic (for evil), too.

Vodun priests can be male (houngan or hungan), or female (mambo). Women Vodun priests are as highly regarded as men, and in some cases held in higher esteem. Women leaders in this religion are generally revered, if not feared.

AFRICAN VOODOO: IT'S NOT WHAT YOU THINK

What do you think of when you hear the word "Voodoo?" Images of witchdoctors and replica dolls with pins stuck in them come to mind, I'll bet. Both images come from Hollywood depictions of South American and Caribbean Voodoo; neither depicts the white magic practiced by African Voodoo followers.

CANDOMBLÉ

Derived from western Africa's Yoruba people, Candomblé seeks harmony and oneness with nature. This religion is organized around high priestesses (or sometimes high priests) and a religious calendar of annual rituals. During religious ceremonies, worshippers dress in colorful garments, place food on the altar, sing special songs, and dance ritualistic steps to the beat of sacred drums. Because these spiritual people think of nature in almost human characteristics, their religion claims to offer intimate contact between the person and the gods. The ultimate Candomblé religious experience occurs when nature and the believer feel like they've become one in spirit.

Countless other religions exist in Africa today, each with customs best suited to its followers, but most of these religions share certain themes: one Almighty Creator who made the world and everything in it, then removed himself to some heavenly realm; belief in an afterlife; belief in a god who punishes, avenges, and rewards; belief in being reunited with (or watched over by) ancestors; and the development of spiritual specialists (healers, weather makers, seers/future tellers, sages, priests). Despite these commonalities between native African religions, two other distinct world religions have penetrated African culture like no other religious following in the land: Christianity and Islam.

During the first centuries a.d., Christianity spread from Asia Minor and the Middle East down over Egypt, into Nubia (south of Egypt), and west to Ethiopia. With the coming of the Prophet Muhammad in the mid-seventh century, Islam spread through northern Africa and then to coastal communities along Arab trading routes.

CHRISTIANITY AND ISLAM IN AFRICA

Centuries later, Christianity and Islam still dominate the religious lives of African peoples. Though some Africans create a religious *hybrid* of old ances-

Muslim African women are often robed.

CHRISTIANITY AND AFRICAN WOMEN

> Jesus Christ, who lived some 2,000 years ago, treated women with dignity and respect unheard of in his day. He taught women, talked with women, welcomed women at his table, and encouraged them to learn.

tral ways and major belief systems (Christianity *and* worship of ancestors, for example), Islam and Christianity are the most widely followed religions on the continent. In Africa, the great Sahara Desert seems to divide the peoples of these faiths: Most Africans of northern and eastern Africa follow Islam; most Africans in central, southern, or western Africa follow Christianity.

When practiced in *moderation*, both religions provide some protections for women. Christianity and Islam, if you read their original teachings, both taught that women and men held equal value, worth, and dignity before God; they just had different roles to fill. Like parts of an automobile engine—both the fuel pump and spark plug are essential and valued, but each performs a different function in making the engine run—women *and* men are important, valued, and necessary. Jesus Christ (the founder and main figure in Christianity) and Muhammad (the central figure of Islam) held higher views of women than the people of their times. Both religions established means for caring for orphans,

widows, and aging parents. Both taught the value of treating one another with gentleness, respect, and love.

Like people in other religions, isolated followers of Christ and some followers of Islam twisted the teachings of their faiths to relegate women to lower status. Christian slave traders bought and sold African nationals on the auction block in ages past. Today's extreme Islamic laws in some countries illustrate just how far these distortions can go.

On September 5, 2000, Sudanese women woke up to find that their freedoms had been removed overnight. Khartoum's governor ordered women in the capital city to stop working in gas stations, hotels, restaurants, and other public places where they might come into direct contact with men. Police, claiming the governor's decree followed Islamic laws (called sharia) that forbid the intermingling of nonmarried or unrelated men and women, ordered working women to stay home or to find jobs where they have no contact with men. Specially empowered police could arrest, fine, or imprison women who disobeyed.

Extreme interpretations of Islam resulted in the violation of women's human rights after the most extreme form of Islamic law, called Sharia, became official in Nigeria. The National Organization for Women, a watch group for women's rights, reported that in January 2001, seventeen-year-old Bariya Ibrahim Magazu was sentenced to one hundred lashes with a cane (an extreme and sometimes-fatal form of whipping) after Muslim authorities discovered she conceived and gave birth to a child out of wedlock the previous year. The girl, who was breast-feeding at the time of her punishment, got pregnant when her father pressured her to have sex with three of his middle-aged friends. The men received no punishment.

Another Islamic court in Nigeria, again applying Sharia law, sentenced a divorced mother of five, Safiya Hussaini Tungar-Tudu, to death by stoning after finding her guilty of having premarital sex and giving birth out of wedlock. A

higher court upheld her death sentence. The man who allegedly raped her was set free because his victim could not produce four eyewitnesses to the rape. Eventually, public outcry won an *acquittal* for this woman, but her case illustrates the inequalities zealously applied religious law can create between the treatment of men and women.

These unfortunate cases are the exception, of course. Very few African nations practice these extreme forms of Islam (though their numbers are on the rise). Many African women, in fact, find religion to be the one place their souls can rise unhindered by the constraints of men. African women, in general, possess deep, abiding faith and belief in the supernatural. African women lead songs of worship in mixed gatherings. Many lead Christian churches, especially in places where wars, AIDS, or *genocides* have killed most adult men. Muslim women are encouraged to practice all *tenets* of the Islamic faith. Some tribal religions set women up as the spiritual leaders.

Religion in the African woman's life can provide a connection with her past, her culture, her heritage, and the supernatural in everyday life. More than superstition, religion in African is *real* to the women who practice it. Sometimes faith was all these women had; and sometimes faith is what gave them strength to work for change.

"WHEN A NEEDLE FALLS INTO A DEEP WELL, MANY PEOPLE WILL LOOK INTO THE WELL, BUT FEW WILL BE READY TO GO DOWN AFTER IT."—AFRICAN PROVERB (GHANA)

REMARKABLE AFRICAN WOMEN
WHO ARE MAKING A DIFFERENCE

Sometimes it seems like too much. Sometimes the job seems too difficult and overwhelming. But all it takes is one person willing to stand for change and great things can happen. Look at what these individuals have done.

WANGARI MUTA MAATHAI (OF KENYA)

Some influential women in Africa worked toward changing people and governments. One woman focused her attention on environmental concerns. What good would women's land ownership rights do her, she reasoned, if pollutants or incessant logging ruined the land she owned? That woman was Wangari Muta Maathai.

The first woman in central or eastern Africa to hold a Ph.D., she was also the first woman to head a university department in Kenya. As head of University of Nairobi's veterinary medicine faculty, she researched veterinary medicine and the effects of environment on animal nutrition. In 1977, she founded the "Green Belt" movement, which has planted over ten million trees. Tree planting prevents soil erosion, replenishes forests, and supplies firewood for cooking.

Wangari Muta Maathai

Women all over Kenya serve as the primary soldiers in the Green Belt movement. African women plant the trees, tend, and water them. They see each tree as an investment in future generations.

Her work to protect Kenya's forests irritated certain government leaders, including Kenya's president, who had her arrested and imprisoned for her protests in 1998. The government released her after worldwide public outcry over her imprisonment. In 1999, opposition forces attacked her while she was planting trees. She suffered head injuries in the attack. But public opinion changed. In 2002, the environmentalist was elected to Kenya's parliament, and was named Kenya's deputy minister in the Ministry of Environment, Natural Resources, and Wildlife shortly after her election.

CONNIE SEKAMANA BWIZA (OF RWANDA)

In 1994, *civil war* between two Rwandan people groups (the Hutus and the Tutsis) created an environment where *radical* Hutus killed an estimated 800,000 Tutsis in mass genocide and slaughtered moderate Hutus who disagreed with them. Connie Sekamana Bwiza helped produce the Arusha Peace Accords—guidelines that encouraged agreement between the warring factions and helped to end Rwanda's civil war. Today she is a member of the Rwandan parliament, where she serves as vice chair of the Forum for Women Parliamentarians.

YINKA JEGED-EKPE (OF NIGERIA)

After she developed a strange rash that just wouldn't go away, the teenage nursing student went to a hospital for a test. When she returned for her results, hospital staff avoided her; no one would talk with her. She soon learned why: her blood work showed signs of HIV (the virus that causes AIDS). She was stunned.

When her nursing schoolteachers found out about her diagnosis, they locked her out of the bathrooms, wouldn't allow her to have patient contact,

tried to expel her, and avoided her. Most of the staff feared she would infect them.

She later learned that she contracted HIV from her dentist's poor sanitation practices (using tainted instruments on multiple patients). Her anger drove her to fight back.

OTHER REMARKABLE AFRICAN WOMEN

Agatha Uwilingiyimana (1953–94) Rwanda's first female prime minister (killed during genocides of 1994)

Ama Ata Aidoo (award-winning writer from Ghana now living in Zimbabwe)

Sylvie Kinigi (banker and first woman prime minister of Burundi 1993–94)

Lorna Kiplagat (Kenyan runner, two-time Los Angeles marathon winner, working to improve training opportunities for Africa's female athletes)

Maria Mutola (current world champion specializing in the 800m track event, four-time Olympian and gold medalist in Sydney in 2000, from Mozambique)

Ama Ata Aidoo, award-winning author.

Lorna Kiplagat, Kenya athlete.

As a nineteen-year-old single Nigerian woman with HIV, Jeged-Ekpe risked being stoned to death if she spoke publicly about her disease. But she knew she had to do something to prevent the same thing from happening to others.

She started with her dentist, demanding that he change his practices to include sanitation procedures and transmission precautions. She promoted widespread public AIDS education. She fought to complete her nursing studies and helped to establish the first People Living with AIDS support group in Nigeria. She became the first woman in Nigeria to speak out about having AIDS. She also established an educational organization called the Nigerian Community of Women Living with HIV/AIDS, which provides specific AIDS information targeted to women and that informs women of their legal rights.

In May, a healthy-looking Yinka Jeged-Ekpe received the 2004 Reebok Human Rights Award for AIDS awareness activism in Nigeria.

IRENE AJAMBO

The last thing the Ugandan female weightlifter needed was to get sick. Even worse, doctors diagnosed her chills and weakness as malaria! Irene Ajambo trains hard nearly every day, but malaria can take the strength out of even the world's best athletes. Olympic trials were under way, and she had to compete no matter how she felt. Despite battling what her coaches call "severe illness," the primary-school-teacher-turned-athlete took three silver medals and one bronze at the 2004 African Weightlifting Championships, earning a place on the Ugandan Olympic Team. Ajambo's efforts proved she is one of an elite group of Ugandan athletes: only ten Ugandan nationals have qualified for the 2004 Summer Games as of this writing. And she earned her spot while fighting off one of the world's deadliest diseases.

Miriam Makeba

WOMEN IN THE WORLD OF AFRICA

MIRIAM MAKEBA

Sometimes called "Mama Africa" or "the Empress of African Song," this gifted vocalist is most recently known for appearing with American recording artist Paul Simon on his Graceland tour in the late 1980s. Few people realized just how vocal this vocalist could be.

Born in 1932 in South Africa, she experienced *apartheid* firsthand. Her powerful voice carried her away from the discrimination of her homeland to recording contracts, international tours, the lead role in a South African musical, and American performance gigs, but her testimony before the United Nations in 1963 might be the strongest, most influential use of her voice in her career. Criticizing her government's racist policies to an international body like the United Nations in that decade cost her her citizenship. She lived in exile in Guinea until the late 1980s. Her voice, along with the blood and voices of her South African brothers and sisters, resulted in the end of apartheid in her homeland. When she returned to South Africa, she went back as a free and equal citizen of her land.

"NO MATTER HOW LONG THE NIGHT, THE DAY IS SURE TO COME."
—AFRICAN PROVERB (CONGO D. R. [ZAIRE])

THE STATUS OF AFRICAN WOMEN TODAY: STILL A LONG WAY TO GO

The United Nations General Assembly Resolution 52/127 states, "Each woman, man and child, to realize their full human potential, must be made aware of all their human rights and fundamental freedoms." Though Africa as a whole is headed in the right direction, several key issues stand in the way of the UN resolution's fulfillment for African women: violence against women, unequal property rights, ongoing wars, and AIDS.

VIOLENCE AGAINST WOMEN

A popular Muslim television host called attention to the seriousness and pervasiveness of spousal abuse by publicly showing her bruised and bloodied face to her nation and the world. In the Islamic world, violence against women, particularly by family members, is a *taboo* subject, largely hidden and never discussed. Broadcast journalist Rania al-Baz, well-known host of a national television magazine show, changed all that when she allowed newspaper photographers to take pictures of her crushed face for publication. After her husband of six years repeatedly thrust her head onto the floor and wall, al-Baz suffered thirteen facial fractures requiring twelve operations.

89

ORGANIZATIONS PROMOTING WORLDWIDE HUMAN RIGHTS

United Nations

Amnesty International

Human Rights Watch

Liberty Human Rights

Physicians for Human Rights

Mary's "husband" regularly beats and rapes her, yet she has never filed a complaint with the police. Why? Mary is a young widow who, by law and custom, was given to her first husband's brother when her first husband died. As far as the police are concerned, her new "husband" has every right to demand sex and obedience from his dead brother's wife; she belongs to him now. Marital rape (forced sexual intercourse between married people) is not a crime in Kenya where Mary lives.

Another Kenyan woman's suffering began when her husband took on a second wife. When she raised questions about the new arrangement, her husband began beating her regularly. He eventually moved out, but he continued to stop by and demand sexual favors. This educated, middle-class woman never went to the police. Kenya law allows wife-beating for just about any reason.

All of these cases, cited by Amnesty International, illustrate the dangers African women face in their own homes. As serious and painful as these situations can be, perhaps the worst violence against women occurs in a practice called "crimes of honor."

Honor crimes occur when someone accuses a woman or teenage girl of compromising her or her family's reputation, and family members assault or kill the accused in order to restore the family's name. A woman can bring shame to her family even if someone simply suggests inappropriate behavior, infidelity, or sexual impurity on her part. Unlike America's justice standard of "innocent until proven guilty," accused women in these cases are found guilty even before they can defend themselves.

One case in northern Africa made headline news in 1997. The Associated Press reported that Marzouk Ahmed Abdel-Rahim, a tile maker from Cairo, Egypt, killed his twenty-five-year-old daughter, Nora, seven days after she eloped with a man her family did not approve. Nora's new husband had previously asked her father for permission to marry Nora, but the older man refused. The young couple ran off and married anyway. Angered by his daughter's act of dishonor, Abdel-Rahim cut off Nora's head and carried it through their neighborhood to display how he had restored his family's honor. He then turned himself into Egyptian police. He served only two months in jail for the brutal murder. *Liberty On-line Magazine* recounts another 1997 attempted Egyptian honor-killing. In a village south of Cairo a father poured gasoline over his nineteen-year-old daughter and set her on fire in an attempt to restore his family's honor after the young girl wed a young man her parents viewed unworthy of her hand in marriage. The girl survived, but the intense heat of the flames left her horribly disfigured.

It isn't just physical violence against women that keeps African women from achieving their dreams; sometimes laws themselves (usually designed to protect citizens) keep women on a lower footing than men. When twelve-year-old girls can be given in marriage to men, their teenage pregnancies keep them out of school, thus hindering any chances of self-improvement. Marriage laws are supposed to protect children, when in reality, in Africa they sometimes justify the practice of early marriage.

The right to own land is another area where African laws have yet to treat women equally. According to most African tribal customs, women can own land only through their husbands, and even then, they have little say in how their husbands use the land. If their husbands die or they divorce, land ownership goes to the husband (in divorce) or to the husband's next of kin (in death). In Kenya, laws state that women cannot inherit land or property. If their husbands or fathers die, the land goes to the next male relative. In the case of a married woman whose husband dies, her in-laws receive her deceased husband's property, and they often evict the widow from her land.

The United Nations *Women's Lands and Property Rights* report includes this testimony (excerpted in part) from a woman living in Rwanda:

> My life has been very bad since my parents died. I had never left my home. I had twelve children on my land. . . . I needed the land so I could . . . look after them. . . . Since my mother's death I have never had access to my forest, nor to my fields.
>
> When I went to court I was told I had lost, even before they started my case. I was not given the chance to speak. When I said I would stay on my father's land, since my father has given it to me, I was put in prison just because I owned my own property. . . . I was badly cut up, and slashed on the head. . . .
>
> Then I met [a woman] and a nice gentleman who listened to me and asked me why I had been chased from my father's land. I asked her organization to defend me as I am looking for justice. . . .
>
> [Her organization] sent someone to my home. He asked my relatives: "Why should she be chased from her father's land? Can a daughter not inherit land? What about all the work she has done? Are you going to pay her for all the work she has done since her youth?" "No," my

WOMEN IN THE WORLD OF AFRICA

A farm in Kenya.

nephews said. "She just has to go." They said no woman has ever inherited land.

Though this woman found help in pleading her case, most women in Africa have little legal recourse when greedy family members take their land from them. These practices seem to affect women in almost all of Africa.

In Lesotho and Swaziland, the law affirms that women cannot own property, enter into contracts, or receive bank loans without being undersigned by a male relative. In Liberia, women cannot inherit property from any male relative (fathers, brothers, husbands, uncles), nor can they own land in their own names.

In Africa, women do more than 70 percent of the agricultural work accomplished there, yet few own the lands on which they toil! And without land, women have little power. Land ownership gives them a place to live, plant crops, graze cattle, and build shelter independently of men. It provides an opportunity and means for a woman to earn income so she can feed herself and her dependents. Without land-ownership rights, women will be forced to stay dependent on men.

A third factor undermines women's advancement in Africa: AIDS.

Seventy percent of all HIV/AIDS cases worldwide occur in sub-Saharan Africa. In Africa, HIV/AIDS infects more than twice as many women as men. Most HIV/AIDS cases in Africa come from heterosexual sexual contact, often husbands to wives.

World Vision, a Christian humanitarian organization, cites these AIDS statistics about Zambia alone:

- At least one hundred Zambians die every day from AIDS.
- One in five Zambian fifteen- to forty-nine-year-olds is infected with HIV/AIDS.

- Because of AIDS, life expectancy has decreased dramatically from 45.5 in 1996 to about thirty-five today.
- Most people in Zambia do not know if they are or are not HIV-infected
- The disease affects the most productive age group of people (between twenty and fifty years of age).
- Approximately half of the 75,000 to 90,000 street children in Zambia are orphans.
- More than half of Zambian children are *chronically* malnourished.
- Four schoolteachers die every day in Zambia.
- AIDS prevalence rates among pregnant women range between 20 and 40 percent.

The numbers get worse when we look at the entire continent. According to the World Health Organization, nearly thirty million men, women, and children in sub-Saharan Africa have HIV/AIDS, three and a half million of which were new cases in 2002. Nearly one in ten African adults has the virus, and nearly 60 percent of these are women. In Africa, AIDS is always eventually fatal.

In a recent address titled *Africa Today and Tomorrow: The Challenges for Women*, Dr. Lieve Fransen, head of the Unit for Social and Human Development, cites these trends:

- Ten times as many people in Africa have died from AIDS than have been killed in wars.
- Young women between the ages of thirteen and twenty-five are the fastest growing group of new cases each year.
- Many of these women have had only one partner, yet contracted HIV from their husbands, or from unwanted sexual contact by rape or assault.

Elaborately hennaed hands.

- Some African myths in rural areas (Swaziland, for example) teach that sex with a young virgin can cure a man of AIDS, which only compounds the number of new cases in young girls each year.

HIV/AIDS is an issue for African women—and not just because it threatens their own lives. In a culture where women are the caretakers, AIDS consumes healthy women's energies and attentions like no other modern issue can.

But this is the bad news. Despite these grim statistics, African women are making headway on other fronts.

ENCOURAGING NEWS FOR AFRICAN WOMEN

The Benin government is taking steps to protect women and children from malaria, a mosquito-born disease that claims more than one million lives around the world each year. Each rainy season brings millions of mosquitoes, and their malaria, to Benin. Mosquitoes bite people, transfer the virus, and the most vulnerable human beings die (mostly pregnant women and young children). The Benin Ministry of Health plans to distribute 240,000 bed nets treated with insecticides to as many pregnant women and children under five as can be contacted by the end of 2004. Though it may not seem like much, this initiative cost $632,000—a sizable investment for the government to make in women's health care needs.

The Ugandan government announced that it will start supplying sanitary napkins to poor students who cannot afford them (just as it does textbooks). These students, who cannot afford their own sanitary supplies, often skip school for the duration of their periods to avoid embarrassment and humiliation. This seemingly small provision will allow teenage girls to attend school without monthly week-long interruptions. The Ministry of Education also expects this provision will help reduce dropout rates for adolescent girls.

March 8 has become International Women's Day and is observed worldwide. It's a day when people around the globe celebrate women's achievements,

are reminded of current needs, and become motivated to work toward securing women's rights everywhere. Publicity surrounding this event keeps women's issues on the forefront of human rights actions throughout the world.

Amnesty International launched its first International Zero Tolerance to Female Genital Mutilation (FGM) Day in February 2004. So far, only fourteen African countries have passed laws prohibiting this practice, but on-going education and awareness continue to chip away at the hold this practice has on so many African cultures.

Across the African continent, women are making gains, both great and small—the right to vote; the right to testify in court; the right to hold office; the right to inherit land; the right to choose a marriage partner; the right to control what happens to her body; the right to pursue education; and to be protected by law. These changes, while allowing for a woman's individual culture and identity, affirm her worth as a human being. They also allow her to celebrate who she is and to become all she was intended to be: a woman in the world of Africa.

FURTHER READING

Aardema, Verna. *The Lonely Lioness and the Ostrich Chicks: A Maasai Tale.* New York: A.A. Knopf; Distributed by Random House, 1996.

Achebe, Chinua. *Things Fall Apart: A Novel.* New York: Anchor, 1994.

Ba Mariama. *So Long a Letter.* Portsmouth, N. H.: Heinemann, 1989.

Bash, Barbara. *Tree of Life: The World of the African Baobab.* San Francisco, Calif.: Little, Brown, 1989.

Dangarembga, Tsitsi. *Nervous Conditions.* New York: Seal, 1988.

Gourevitch, Philip. *We Wish to Inform You That that Tomorrow We Will Be Killed with Our Families: Stories from Rwanda.* New York: Picador USA, 1998.

McCord, Margaret. *The Calling of Katie Makanya: A Memoir of South Africa.* New York: John Wiley & Sons, 1998.

Mungoshi, Charles. *Stories from a Shona Childhood.* Bedminster, N.J.: Baobab, 1989.

Oduyoye. Mercy Amba. *Daughters of Anowa: African Women and Patriarchy.* Maryknoll, N. Y.: Orbis, 1995.

Oju, Dympna Ugwu. *What Will My Mother Say: A Tribal African Girl Comes of Age in America*. Chicago, Ill.: Bonus, 1995.

Steptoe, John. *Mufaro's Beautiful Daughters: An African Tale*. New York: Lothrop, Lee & Shepard, 1987.

Thiong'o, Ngugi wa. *A Grain of Wheat*. Portsmouth, N.H.: Heinemann, 1994.

Vera, Yvonne. *Butterfly Burning*. Bedminster, N.J.: Baobab, 1998.

Wassef, Hind. *Daughters of the Nile: Photographs of Egyptian Women's Movements, 1900–1960*. Cairo, Egypt: American University in Cairo, 2001.

FOR MORE INFORMATION

Africa
www.pbs.org/wnet/africa

Africa Online: Kids
www.africaonline.com/AfricaOnline/coverkids.html

African Lives—Washington Post
www.washingtonpost.com/wp-srv/inatl/longterm/africanlives/front.htm

African Peoples Resources
www.uiowa.edu/~africart/toc/people.html

Africawoman Online
www.africawoman.net

Afrol.com—Women
www.afrol.com/Categories/Women/msindex.htm

Life in Africa
www.lifeinafrica.com

The Living Africa: The People
library.thinkquest.org/16645/ the_people/the_people.shtml

Minnesota Science Museum's Greatest Places: Namib Page
www.sci.mus.mn.us/greatestplaces/book_pages/namib2.htm

Motherland Nigeria: Kidzone
www.motherlandnigeria.com/kidzone.html

Okavango Delta Peoples of Botswana
anthro.fullerton.edu/jbock/Okavango

People of Africa
www.princetonol.com/groups/iad/ lessons/middle/people.htm

The Story of Africa
www.bbc.co.uk/worldservice/africa/features/storyofafrica

United Nations Women Watch
www.un.org/womenwatch

WomensNet—Zaire
womensnet.org.za

Publisher's note:
The Web sites listed on these pages were active at the time of publication. The publisher is not responsible for Web sites that have changed their addresses or discontinued operation since the date of publication. The publisher will review and update the Web sites upon each reprint.

GLOSSARY

acquittal Finding a criminal defendant not guilty of the charge against him/her.

activist Someone who acts in support of something.

affirmative action A program that gives advantage to a group of people to make up for previous discrimination.

anthropologists Scientists who study the behavior, culture, and social development of human beings.

apartheid The policy of segregation and political and economic discrimination against people of non-European races.

archaeologists Scientists who study the relics, artifacts, and monuments of past human life and activities.

chronically To occur long term or recur frequently.

civil war A war between opposing groups of citizens of the same country.

constitution The document recording the basic principles and laws of a nation.

cooperative An organization owned by and operated for the benefit of those using its services.

entrepreneur Someone who organizes, manages, and takes on the risks of a business.

genocides The deliberate destruction of a racial, political, or cultural group.

homogenous Made up of the same or similar nature.

hybrid Something new created from two diverse items.

matriarchs Female leaders.

midwife A trained, nonphysician who performs medical procedures for women; often assisting in childbirth.

moderation Not done to an extreme—not too much, not too little.

nomadic Roaming about from place to place.

paradox Something that is seemingly contradictory.

pawpaws Fleshy fruits similar in appearance to mangoes.

radical Something that departs significantly from the usual or the traditional.

satellite schools Educational facilities away from traditional sites, often to accommodate nontraditional students.

savannahs Tropical or subtropical grasslands containing scattered trees and drought-resistant undergrowth.

subservient Being placed or used in an inferior position.

taboo Forbidden.

tenets Principles, beliefs, and doctrines generally held to be true.

INDEX

PICTURE CREDITS

Artville: p. 6; Michelle Bouch: pp. 22, 80, 83, 84, 86, 91; Corbis: pp. 72, 74, 76, 99; Corel: cover, pp. 12, 15, 16, 26, 29, 30, 33, 39, 40, 43, 45, 48, 51, 42, 56, 59, 64, 67, 68, 71, 92, 95, 96; Map Resources: cover; Benjamin Stewart: cover.

BIOGRAPHIES

Joan Esherick is a full-time author and freelance writer who lives with her family outside Philadelphia, Pennsylvania. She's authored fifteen books, including *Our Mighty Fortress: Finding Refuge in God* (Moody Press, 2002), *The Big Picture: The Bible's Story in Thirty Short Scenes,* and multiple texts with Mason Crest Publishers. Joan has also contributed dozens of articles to national print periodicals. For more information about her, you can visit her Web site at www.joanesherick.com.

Dr. Mary Jo Dudley is the director of Cornell University's Gender and Global Change Department, which focuses on the evolving role of gender around the world. She is also the associate director of Latin American Studies at Cornell.